# Elephants

## A Colouring Book Journey to Enlightenment

(QB Books)

Relax and unwind with these beautiful Elephant illustrations to colour and enjoy.

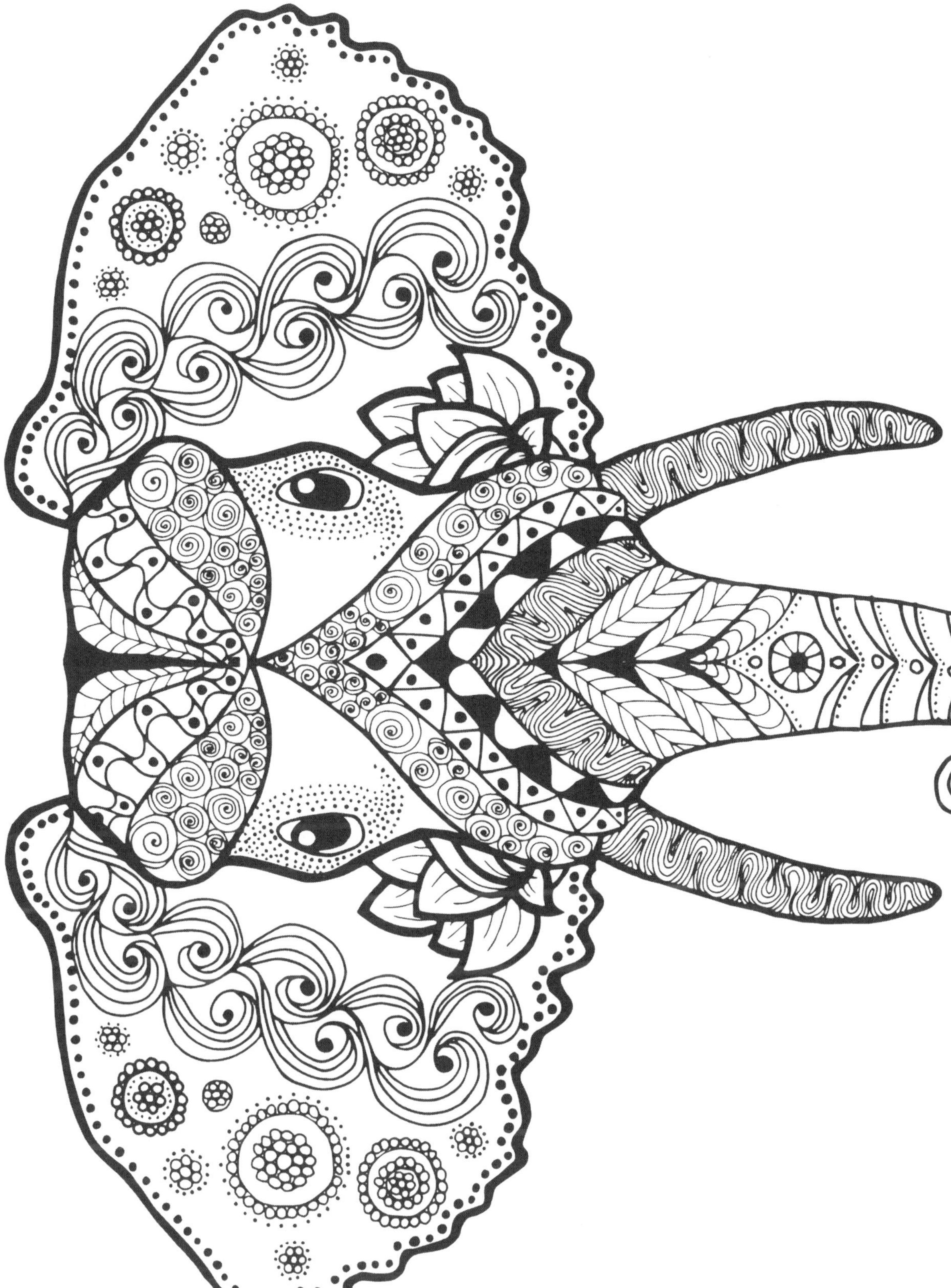

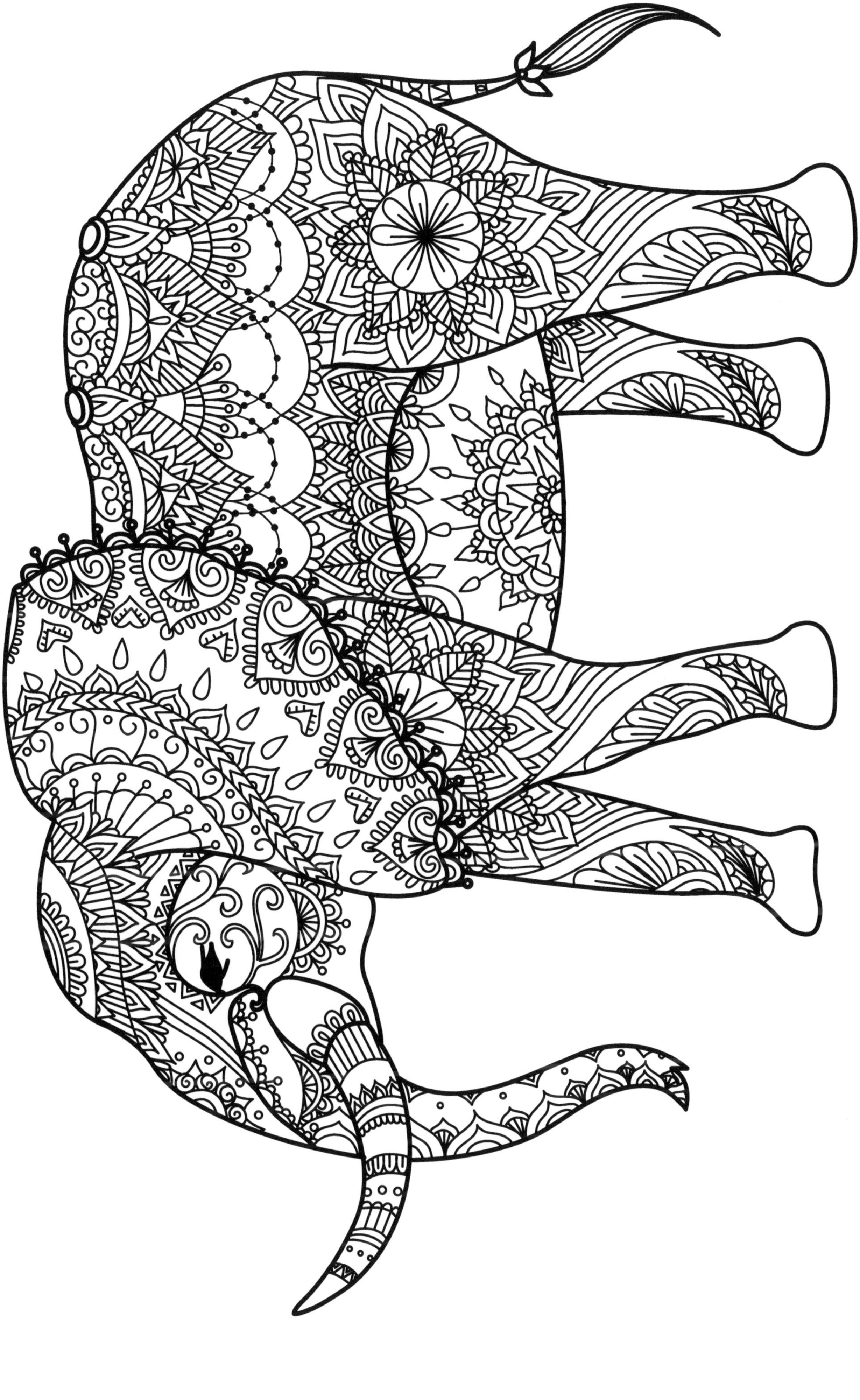

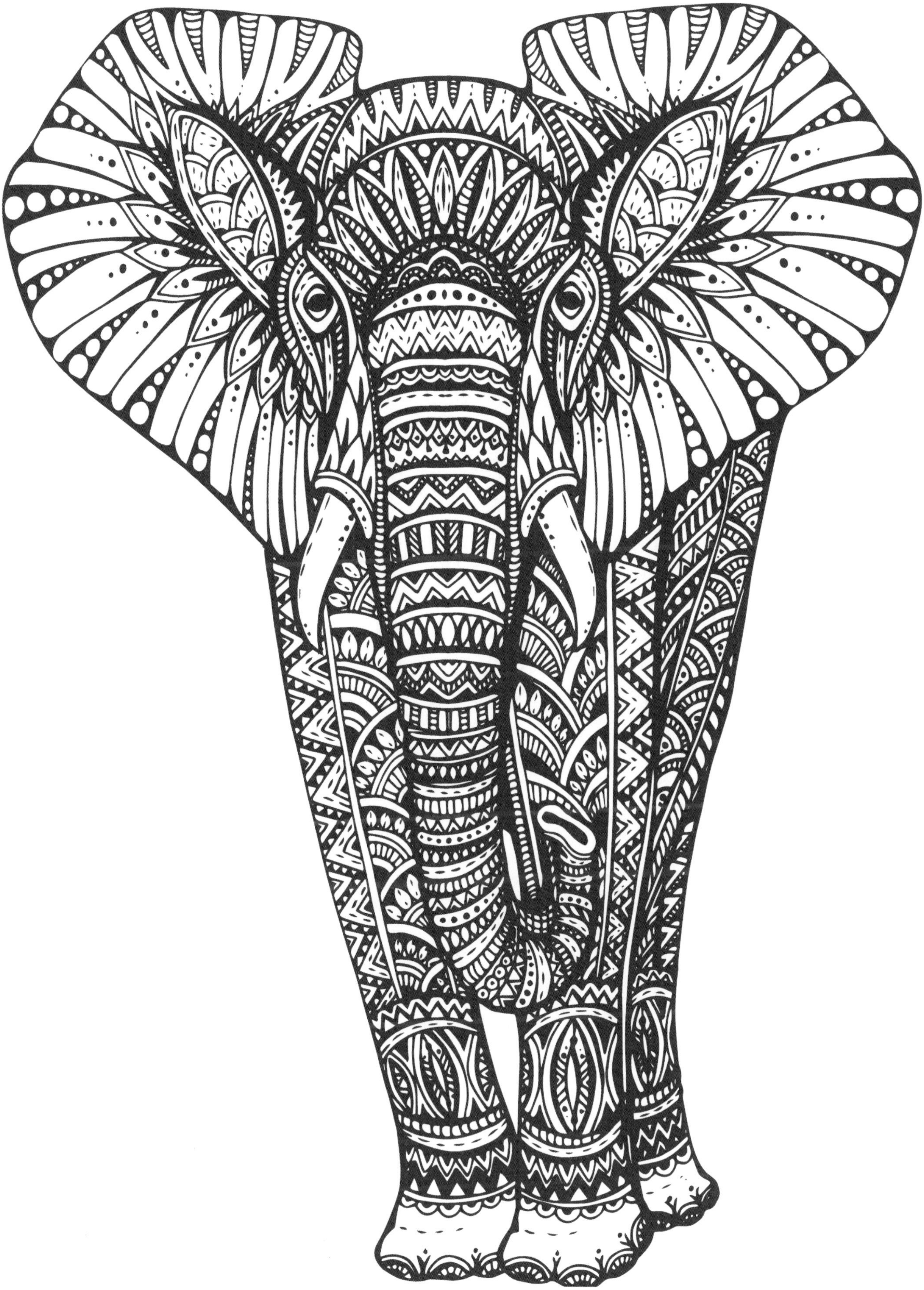

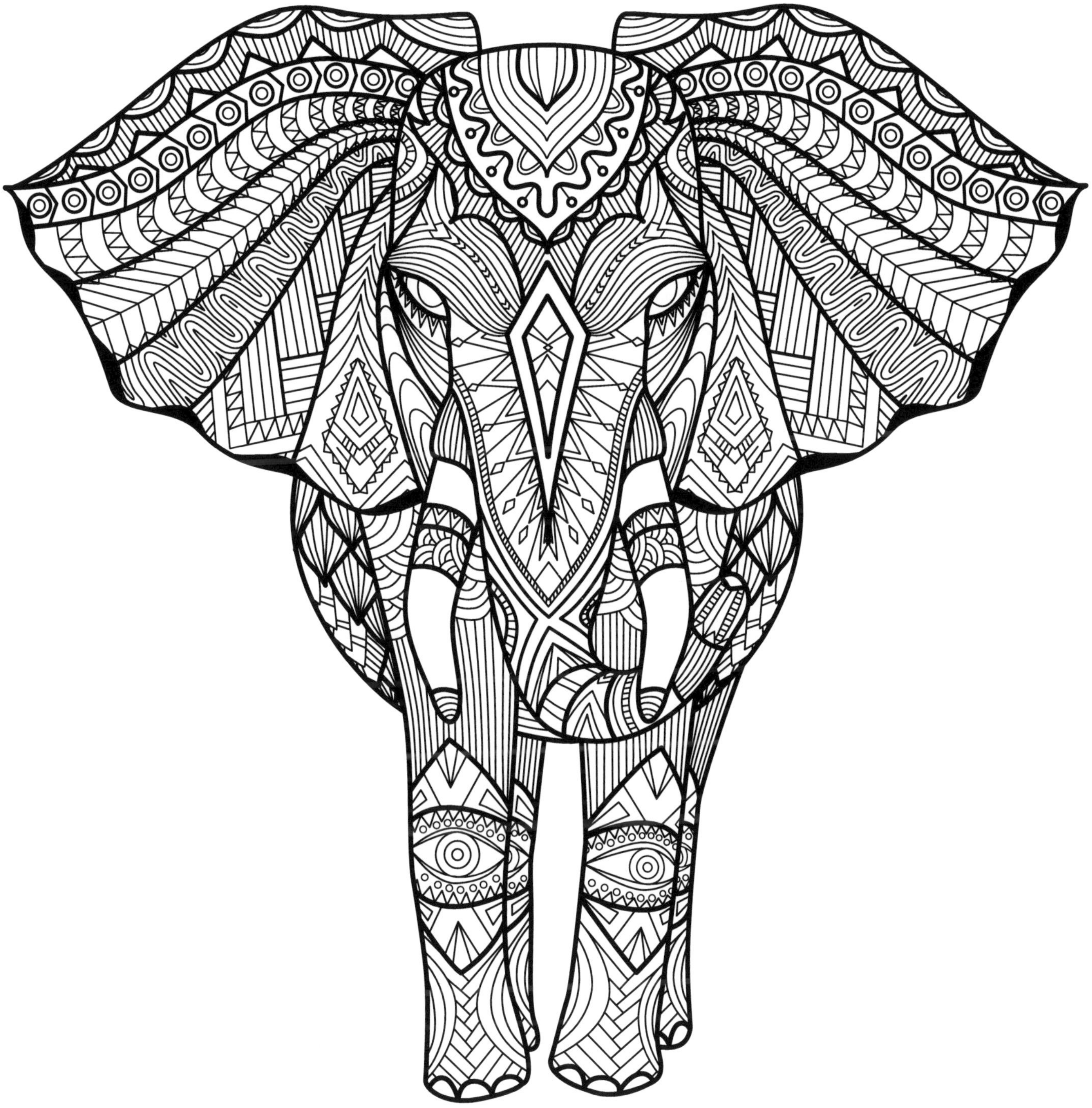

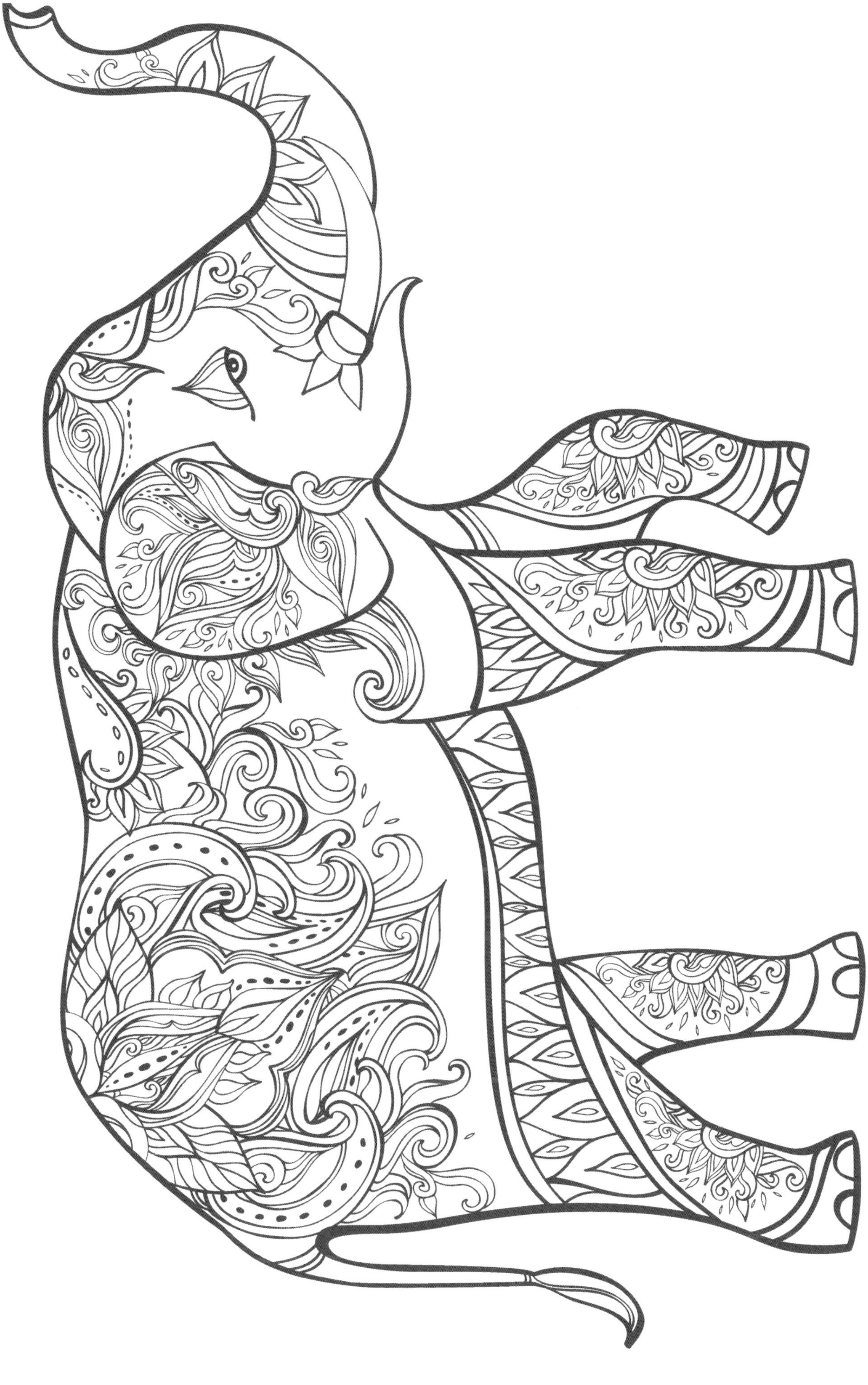

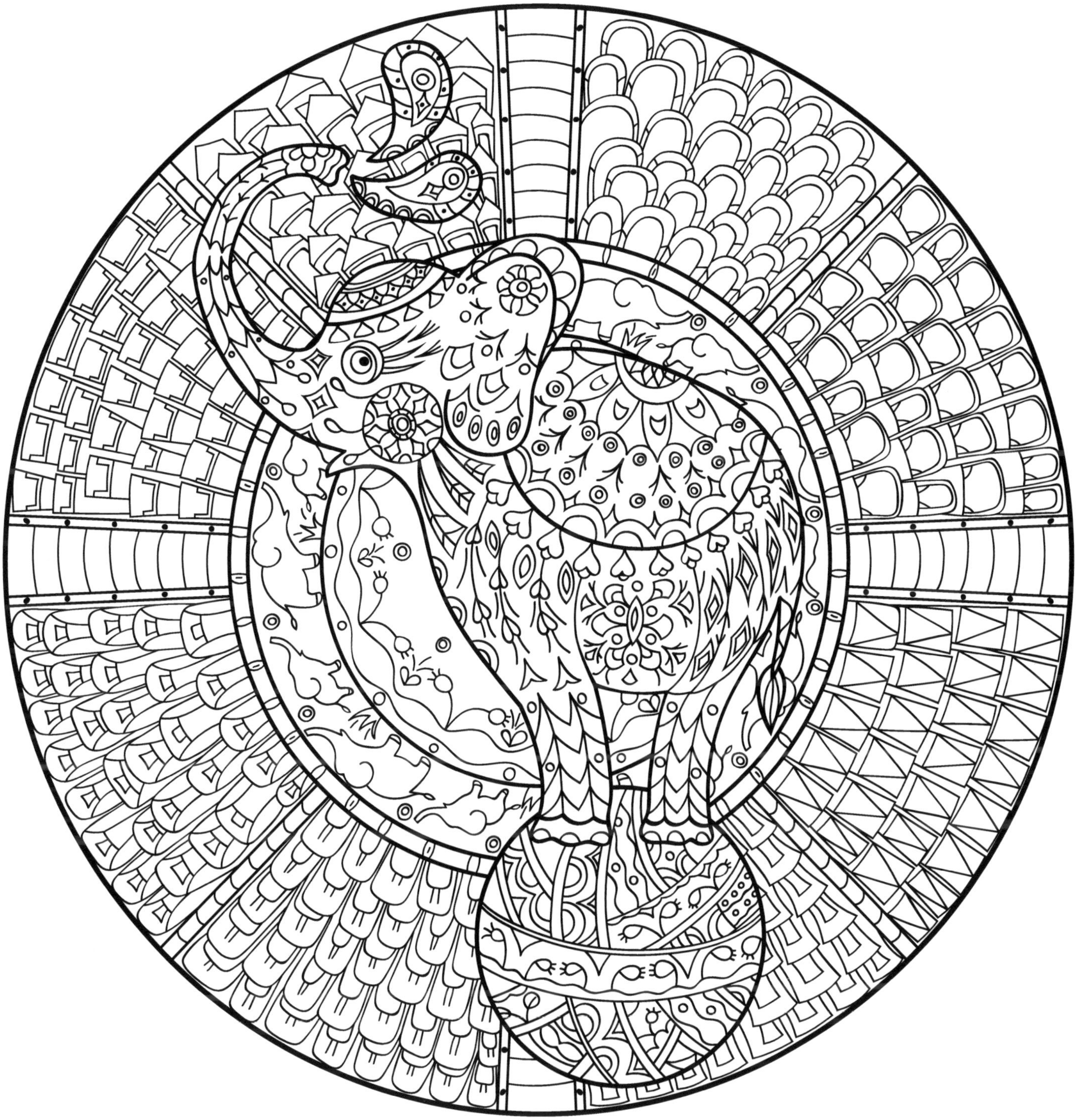

24898644R00046

Printed in Great Britain
by Amazon